The Work of Manifestation:
Rituals, Crystals, Herbs, Oils & Baths to Create the Abundant Life You Deserve

The Art of Manifestation Series

By Rev. Mignon Grayson
Sacred Mysteries World Wide, LLC

The Work of Manifestation:
Rituals, Crystals, Herbs, Oils & Baths to Create the Abundant Life You Deserve

Rev. Mignon Grayson

Copyright © 2020
United States Copyright Office

All Rights Reserved. No part of this publication may be reproduced, distributed, or transmitted in any form or by any means, including photocopying, recording, or other electronic or mechanical methods, without the prior written permission of the publisher, except in the case of brief quotations embodied in reviews and certain other noncommercial uses permitted by copyright law. Disclaimer: This book is designed to provide accurate and authoritative information in regard to the subject matter covered. By its sale, neither the publisher nor the author is engaged in rendering psychological or other professional services. If expert assistance or counseling is needed, the services of a competent professional should be sought.

TABLE OF CONTENTS

Introduction	5
Energy, Vibration, Frequency	8
The Benefits of The Assisting Modalities	9
Benevolent Spirits' Assistance	10
Manifesting Rituals & Ceremonies	15
The Rituals	19
Guided Meditation (Self-Hypnosis)	34
Spiritual Bathing	39
Abundance Manifestation Herbs	41
Other Types of Rituals	45
Additional Manifestation Tools	48
Energy…Again	54
Potentiality & The Gateway Of Manifestation	57
Putting It Altogether	59
Conclusion	60

DEDICATION

This book is dedicated to Olodumare / Ntr / God, my Ancestors, my Spirit Guides, my spiritual Elders, and to Onile (earth) for the life and inspiration that flows through me. This book is gift from them. May I always continue to receive their blessings as I walk upon this earth.

This book is also dedicated to You, the Reader. May you discover the beauty, uniqueness and power of your Spirit and realize your ultimate potential and ability to co-create your life with the Creator.

INVOCATION

Infinite energy within, infinite energy without.

Constant, continuous, never ending.

Energy transforms, energy transmutes.

Manifesting.

Invisible essence, substance of every visible form.

Conscious union with this invisible Life,

Connecting to earth, water, fire, air and ether

To bring forth soul imaginings and manifest creative thinking

Life is infinite energy coupled with limitless creative thought.

Infinite energy is me, infinite energy is you.

All of life is infinite energy.

Abundance is a flow of infinite energy through you.

Abundance is you manifesting.

INTRODUCTION

This book is written as a companion book to its predecessor, "The Art of Manifestation: Simple Energy Techniques to Create the Abundant Life You Deserve." This book stands alone but can work in harmony with the overarching principles and techniques in the first book. The first book goes into detail about the energetic principles of manifesting. Used together or separately, you will achieve the same aim. My first book focuses on using personal energy, mental and emotional clearing and conditioning. This book is mainly focused on external modes of energy and the ritual process that when paired with your personal energy will enhance manifestation.

The Art of Manifestation is a process by which through the application of certain energy techniques you can bring into being the things and circumstances you desire. The Law of Attraction and Quantum Mechanics are essential tools of the Manifestation Art. They are the more popular in the spiritual arena. They are the principles that are at work in the techniques provided in this book

First and foremost, all of the techniques provided in this book are energetic extensions of you, the practitioner (Manifestor). You are a powerful being capable of co-creation with the Universe. You can manifest using only your mind and personal energy alone. You are an extension of the Divine and are imbued with divinity. As such, you are capable of original Divine thought which is the catalyst that brings things into being. However, we are not taught this in our early years and so we are unaware of who we truly are at the core of our being. We are out of touch and definitely out of practice. Manifestation techniques are designed to put you in touch with your core essential energy, and as such, you begin to relearn who you are. You begin to remember and get in touch with your Divine essence. With each successful manifestation, it confirms your truest identity. This is the main benefit of embarking on the manifestation process. The things or circumstances you acquire through manifestation as your original intended goal, are merely by products of the realization of your personal power and essential being. This brings awareness of your connection to the Divine in profound ways.

The techniques in this book are physical energy practices that will enhance your manifestation work. I call them "assisting modalities." Because we are externally focused and easily distracted, the strength and potency of our energy vacillates from day to day. Using the assisting modalities in this book will ensure that the energy level of your manifestation work keeps at a certain intensity even when you are not able to give it as much energy as usual. Important to the success of manifestation is the application of sustained energy and focus. These assisting modalities are your backup generator. Additionally, for those who appreciate ritual and ceremony, this can add diversity and fun to the manifestation work.

My first book, *"The Art of Manifestation: Simple Energy Techniques to Create the Abundant Life You Deserve,"* included the techniques of scripting, "Act As If," meditation, visualization, breathwork, and water manifestation. Included in this book will be more manifestation techniques and rituals, herbs and spiritual baths that will add to the toolbox. Included techniques are the Quantum Jumping Water Technique, 17:3-6-9 Method, and a Guided Meditations specific for manifestation. There will also be a section that gives suggested routines and how to combine techniques for optimum results.

ENERGY, VIBRATION, FREQUENCY

Throughout the book the terms energy, vibration and frequency will be used often. Everything comes down to the utilization of one form or another of this vital substance. Herbs, crystals, prayers, affirmations, moon phases, planets, stars, etc. all contain energy at varying rates of frequency. This books details how to utilize them to enhance your manifestation work. This book will guide you on how to activate these various modes of energy and how to combine them with each other for maximum results.

As you are actively working on manifesting, there are important occurrences happening: you are learning how to bring through the energy you desire in your life and you're also nurturing your own energy in order to do this. You are growing energetically. You are enhancing your own personal power. Innately, you are learning the energetic realm in the process. You are encountering the inner realms and opening yourself up to a deeper understanding. The long-term benefits of this are many and lasting. You are growing spiritually.

In ancient times, the spiritual gatekeepers intuited the energies of things within their environment and determined what they could be used for to balance, heal and enhance their community and also to deepen spiritual experiences. Their uses were confirmed through application, trial and error. When you're spiritually in tune, you will be able to recognize energy signatures and be able to tap into the "universal mind" and get the information needed. The uses of the items included in this book have been proven through the tests of time. They are selected and compiled with care. In our world of information technology, there is a wealth of information that you have access to. There are many ways to achieve manifestation. I have taken the time to assemble with experience and care the information in this book so that a newbie or seasoned practitioner can benefit.

THE BENEFITS OF THE ASSISTING MODALITIES

As mentioned previously, in doing manifestation work all that is essential is your inner work. Your ability to tap into your inner realm and manage your mental and energetic landscapes is what is most important. What should be emphasized, is people are easily distracted. Our energy levels vacillate day to day, hour to hour, and minute by minute so we can't always rely on the level of our concentration and energy reserves to effectively fuel our manifestation work. Even with someone who is always upbeat and pleasant and usually in positive state of mind, there are times when they aren't able to be in that positive space as easily. Adding rituals, symbols, herbs, incense and oils to your manifestation work will assist you in getting into the most potent frame of mind. They act as energy containers and energetic triggers. Combining these practices with any type of manifestation work makes shifting into the states of awareness extremely conducive for manifesting, readily achievable. Rituals and ceremonies require carving out time in your schedule to allow for extended time to focus. Rituals, herbs, incenses and oils not only bring their added energetic frequencies that help to strengthen what you are doing, they also awaken your five senses to the process which in turn bolsters your energetic focus. For those who are ritually inclined, this adds an extra feeling of enjoyment and total surrender to your manifestation work.

Another point to mention is that everyone perceives and experiences things in differently through the senses. It has been scientifically proven that people take in information and process their emotions based on having an emphasis on one or two of the 5 primary senses. There are those that are auditory-hearing (music, affirmations, prayers), visual-sight (reading sacred text, candles, sigils, symbols), feelings, or tactile/touch (environment, altars, ritual & ceremony process, oils and spiritual baths) and olfactory- smell (oils, incenses, spiritual baths) inclined. Everyone is more inclined to one or another. Creating ritual and ceremony combines all of them at one time.

There are many benefits to incorporating all or some of these additional tools. I enjoy using every one of them in my manifestation work. It allows me the opportunity to create a space and time to be creative and to ignite my senses towards a higher purpose.

BENEVOLENT SPIRITS' ASSISTANCE

We have the ability to call on benevolent spirits whose job and desire it is to help us grow, develop and reach our goals and dreams. There are different types and I will discuss the three that I feel are the most relevant when it comes to manifestation. They are your Ancestors, Spirit Guides and Archangels (they go by other names in other traditions such as Orisha, Devi, Abosum, Neteru.)

When engaging in spiritual endeavors, it is important to enlist the guidance and help of these evolved spirits. The Benevolent Spirits act as "spiritual sponsors" because they are the residents of spiritual realm. They know how to best navigate it in order to bring results to your manifestation work. When you are making spiritual requests and moving spiritual energy to manifest, having them aligned will bring higher quality to your manifestations. Direct requests from you to them bring stronger results. They are also ready to give guidance and help you elevate your thoughts about your life and the direction you are going. They are also here to protect you against adverse energies and spiritual attacks.

Because you are incarnated into a physical body, you have certain limitations within the material realm. The benevolent spirits do not have these limitations and can provide assistance and boost the energy that you are putting out into the universe to manifest. They will also provide guidance on what you are doing and will also alert and inspire you to seize opportunities that otherwise you wouldn't recognize or acknowledge. This guidance comes in many forms: inspirational thoughts, ideas, whisperings, mental pictures, strong feelings. They may also provide messages to you on the Manifestation methods you are using to modify them to better work for you… the methods are numerous. Pay attention as you work with some of these rituals for messages about adding or removing different elements. That is why it is important to pray and call on your Spirit Guides, Ancestors and Archangels before, during, or after every ritual to ensure their strong presence is with you and working on your behalf. Follow the guidance should you receive any.

For the purpose of this book, I will only concentrate on the Ancestors, Spirit Guides, and Archangels since they are familiar to most people in the western hemisphere and across the world. The Orisha, Devi, Abosum and Neteru are culturally specific and require knowledge from elders within the cultural tradition to properly call upon them.

Ancestors are your family members who have lived and died before or during your lifetime. The Ancestors we want to be by our side are the ones who are elevated. Ancestors want us to thrive and do well in life. They understand the ups and downs and ins/outs of this life and can provide comfort, guidance and assistance with knowledge and wisdom. Calling on them to assist you with everyday life as well as asking them to bless your manifestation work is as simple as calling them by name. They are always around and ready to assist. As a matter of fact, they are already assisting you in the ways that they can. Certain of your Ancestors hold expertise from when they were alive. If you are working or studying a particular Ancestor's field of expertise, you can ask her/him to provide assistance and insight. If you don't know any names of your Ancestors, you can generally call them by saying "elevated ancestors of my mother's side, elevated ancestors of my father's side. Ancestors' messages can come through dreams or intuition. Call on the Ancestors in your family that lived a good and decent life while on earth. This guarantees they are doing the same while in the spirit realm. Some people have an Ancestral altar setup in their home. If you do, you can sit with them at the altar to enlist their help with manifesting your desires. If you want to know how to setup an Ancestral altar, you can visit our Youtube channel: at:
https://www.youtube.com/channel/UCpgEudpK0Rhs3KaPii7ZIaw

For more information on Ancestor Reverence and Connection, you can visit the Sacred Mysteries website and read the blog article on ancestors. Visit www.sacredmysteries.org.

Spirit Guides are exactly what the name says… Spirits that provide guidance. They can also be an Ancestor but more than likely are an elevated Spirit who was assigned to you at birth and is invested in your wellbeing, especially your spiritual evolution and ascension. This Spirit has elevated to a position of Guide through their own personal spiritual growth. Through meditation you can learn to connect with your Spirit Guide. They also are always around you ready to assist. They have already been assisting you all along. Taking steps to get closer to them ensures that we receive their guidance more directly and fully.

Most of the Archangels are spirits that have not incarnated and who the Divine has given certain powers and abilities in order to keep the Universe, earth and people in balance. They are very powerful. They prefer to work within the laws of the Universe but can operate outside of them if necessary.

Here is a list of the Archangels from Christianity that assist with manifesting prosperity, abundance and related circumstances. If they resonate with you, call of them to help with your manifestation work:

- **Archangel Ariel:** Prosperity is under this angel's domain. Ariel will guide you to the ways of increased wealth every area of life. She helps find employment, in business endeavors. Ariel will remind you of your worth. She will show you how to be open to all of the prosperity and abundance you deserve. With her assistance prosperity can come from both expected and unexpected sources. Helps with transitions for the arrival of what you have been manifesting.
- **Archangel Barakiel:** Angel of Blessings. He helps to align you with your highest destiny and the blessings contained therein. He assists in connecting you with your inner joy and gratitude which accelerates the manifestation of your desires for your highest good.
- **Archangel Chamuel:** Confidence booster so that you can, build career success. He will assist you with clearer thinking so that you can be able to identify areas of blockages to the flow of prosperity.

- **Archangel Hamied:** Bringer of miraculous experiences. Restorer of faith in miracles, magic and the ability to call forth abundance from them. Archangel of Miracles.
- **Archangel Haniel:** Helps with igniting your passion in your life. She heals emotional wounds which may hinder your progress. She will bring opportunities and people that are for your highest good.
- **Archangel Metatron:** Brings in to focus your soul mission, passions, and desire to create positive change. He assists in tapping into skills and resources you developed in over many lifetimes.
- **Archangel Michael:** Archangel of Protection and Courage. Enhances your personal strength. Protects and removes blockages of negative energy clearing the way to manifest abundance and your dreams.
- **Archangel Pathiel:** Opens the Gates of positive Manifestation. His name means "the opener." He is the one to call on if you want to open the gates of manifestation to bring the creation of abundance and prosperity. Call upon him and let him know your desires. Write a petition/list and ask Pathiel for the path to your wishes and desires to open so that they can easily manifest into your life. Then surrender your list to Pathiel. Trust that your prayers have been heard and have already been answered.
- **Archangel Raziel:** Archangel of Divine Magic. He helps tap into your inner magical energy to bring forth manifestation of your desires. He helps to manifest prosperity. He will reveal the mysteries of the Universe when you're ready. This can bring to your mind Divinely inspired income generating ideas.
- **Archangel Zacharael:** Helps you to surrender and release destructive tendencies and experiences which may be blocking your prosperity. He will also assist you in letting go of addictions and attachments.

Because Pathiel deals directly with the topic of this book, Manifestation, I will include a prayer specific to Pathiel:

Prayer to Pathiel

Pathiel, you are the one who rules over manifestation. You have the power to manifest abundance and prosperity for my highest good. Assist me in opening the gates of manifestation so everything good and beneficial can flow freely and easily into my life. I recite then surrender my petition to you. I know you are the one who can accomplish this for me. I trust in you. I trust that my prayers have already been answered.

Archangels are extremely benevolent and helpful when called upon for assistance. Call upon them just before or after you have engaged in manifestation work to add their blessings.

MANIFESTING RITUALS & CEREMONIES

All of the following suggestions can be done in ritual or ceremonial style. The only difference is that ritual can be solitary and up to as many people as desired, but usually a small, intimate group. A ceremony is usually for a group of 4 or more people.

Be Clear About What You Want

Before beginning any ritual, it is best to prepare by having clear ideas of what you want to manifest. Write them out. Make a list. Choose one that is a priority for you. In the beginning, aim for smaller goals. This will ensure as a beginner that you have achievements early on. You will then become more confident. You also become seasoned and accustomed to the process and comfortable with the way in which you work the energies. Quality over quantity is always the best approach.

Ritual Prep: Approaching Your Ritual/Ceremony

Make sure you have all that you need gathered together. Mentally prepare by going into a meditative state and envisioning what you are going to do. Bless your intentions. Place yourself in a state that radiates reverence and gratitude for the Divine. Call on your Spirt Guides, Ancestors, Archangels to bless your ritual and to be by your side and guide and protect you. When you approach your ritual or ceremony, it is important to release all tension and any anxiety. Breathing is a great tool for this. Use EFT (Emotional Freedom Technique) if you are familiar. EFT uses tapping on various parts of your body to achieve calm. There are many resources online.

Cleanse the area where you are doing the ritual with either incense (frankincense & myrrh, sweet grass, sage, Palo Santo, or any other incense you use for this purpose) or splash/spray with a spiritual water such as Florida Water, Kananga Water or you can make your own. This will disperse any unwanted and unhelpful energies that may be lingering around. You can play music from your manifesting playlist or any relaxing music to help get you in the mood. Please note, for a ceremony involving more than you and a couple of other people, setting up the ceremonial space before others arrive is a good idea. You can invite a few people to arrive earlier if you need help setting up for a larger group. All of the major setup (including ritual cleansing) should be done before the entire group arrives.

At whatever point feels best, invoke your energetic tools (as discussed in my earlier book) into your ritual/ceremony to strengthen and support the effectiveness of your manifestation ritual/ceremony. Get settled. Delve into the power of your conscious and subconscious mind. Tap into the frequency of that which you desire. Step into the realm of potentiality. Performing these rituals and ceremonies help you to strengthen your focus and channel your energetic processes for manifestation. A group dynamic further strengthens everyone's energetic input by the increased potency of everyone's energy.

In a ceremonial setting there should be 1 to 3 people who lead the group from one segment to the next to ensure everyone is on the same page at the same time. The format can loosely be the following: Opening prayers, consecration of the ritual space, invocation of the Ancestors and Spirit Guides to bless the event, libation (for those who do this as part of their path), meditation, manifestation ritual, closing prayers, giving thanks and releasing ancestors and spirit guides.

The Abundance Rule: Harm None

At this point I will mention the rule "harm no one". What you are manifesting should not be something that belongs to another that you want to take away and should not be an effort to sway a particular person to be with you, as you must always respect another's free will. Doing intentional harm will backfire. Refrain from this immediately.

Maintaining a Powerful Ritual

Work with the rituals that you are drawn to. Do not force yourself to do something just because it has been provided to you. There are several different types of rituals in this book so that you can choose which one(s) are appealing to you. Aversion and resistance to a ritual diminishes the potency.

A great ritual enhancer is your ability to meditate and concentrate. Work on your ability to focus throughout the day. Commit to focusing on one thought or task without distraction for 2-5 minutes periodically throughout the day. Other enhancers are spending time journaling, praying, gratitude work, communing with nature and physical activity (yoga and tai chi are great!) Breathwork is really important. Breathing exercises improve and increase your personal energy (chi, kundalini, ki, ab).

Starting with small manifestation goals is a great way for you to get comfortable and to have successes that build your confidence level. A confident mindset is very helpful to this art.

For each manifestation ritual that you decide to embark on, determine the length of time you will commit to it. Customary durations are usually 3, 5, 7 days or 30-day commitments. This means committing to putting energy into manifestation daily for that length of time. It is entirely up to you how you want to shape your schedule and commitment. Doing the same things every day will strengthen and supercharge the energy field building it up over time. Also note, best times to engage are early morning when you first wake up and just before you go to sleep. Your brainwaves are at optimum level to absorb what you are programming into your mind and spirit for manifestation.

This is sacred time that you should honor and commit to it as such. Your family, loved ones and roommates should be aware not to disturb you.

THE RITUALS

Ritual 1
Cleansing

A great way to embark on your manifestation journey is to initiate it with a cleansing ritual that will remove accumulated negative spiritual energy that may be with you. These unwanted energies can block the positive manifestations you are calling in. They can also weigh you down and make you feel less interested in making this very uplifting step in elevating your life. A spiritual cleansing creates a clean energetic slate which is ideal to start.

The goal: to reset and to break away from any potentially stagnant energies, clearing the way for easier manifestations

Timing: New moon cycle OR whenever you feel you are entering a new cycle (new job, new relationship, new home, new school)

Frequency: Monthly / When you feel the need

Duration: Once or 2 to 3 consecutive days

What you need: Bowl/container of water, white flowers, Florida Water, essential oil of basil and lavender. *(if you are sensitive to essential oils you can leave them out or use 5 drops instead of 10)*

Take a cleansing/uplifting spiritual bath. Combine in 2-quarts of water, petals from white flowers, 2 or 3 splashes of Florida Water, 10drops of essential oil of basil and lavender in a basin or bowl. Take a regular shower or bath. Stand in the tub or shower and pour the prepared bath over you from the neck down, back and front, while praying for cleansing, peace, protection and tranquility. Dry off and put on clean, white or light-colored clothing, sit in front of your altar (or anywhere that allows for meditation), light a white candle. Call on your spirit guides/ancestors to help you disconnect from any negativity that is around you and to put a protective shield around you by visualizing a white radiant light surrounding you and illuminating all the darkness. The light emanates from above and comes down all around you. Read an inspirational passage in your favorite book of sacred text, poetry, etc. Relax and proceed with 1 to 3 cycles of the cleansing breath. Proceed with a meditation to cleanse your auric field and connect with your Higher Self. This meditation enables you to connect with your inner source that is always at a state of "zero" where all things manifest from (primordial energy.) Once complete, say a closing prayer. You are now ready to proceed to either do a new manifestation process discussed later in the book, or you can take this relaxed time to journal about the cleansing experience and how starting fresh feels.

Ritual 2
Clear Negativity by Fire

The goal: to release built-in negative conditions/subconscious programming to allow for manifestations

Timing: Full Moon Cycle / Whenever you feel the need

Frequency: Monthly or When you feel the need

What You Need: Cleansing Bath, Pen, 2 Sheets of Paper, Lighter, Fireproof Container

Take a strong cleansing bath (bath/shower first). You can use the one in the previous ritual as a base. To make it a bit stronger, add a few drops of rosemary essential oil. Dress in comfortable light-colored clothing, dark clothing is ok too, but not black. Sit in front of your altar (or anywhere that allows for meditation), light a colored candle of your choosing, or black. Set your mood for going within. Say any opening prayers that put you in touch with your inner realm/spirit. Call on your Spirit Guides or Ancestors to set a protective circle around you. Call on them to also help you recognize what you are holding on to that is blocking you from allowing your abundance to manifest in your current reality. Ask them to make it clear what needs to be let go--especially that which you may be in denial about. Sit quietly, be still and listen. Let your attention go where you are led by your intuition. Write it down.

Each time something stands out, write it down. Number each item. You can also add to the list all that you already know you have to let go. Once you feel you have put all that you need to on the list. Take out your second sheet of paper. Go back to the beginning of the list. Internally, read each item one at a time (do not read them out loud as spoken word adds power.) On the new sheet of paper, write the reverse of each item -- a positive statement. Complete the positive list. Put it to the side. Take the 1st list and go from the first to the last item, putting a line through each one and saying internally or out loud "this is no longer true for me. It never was." If you want to add extra energy into releasing what is on the list, you can stand and place the list on the floor. Step on the list. Stomp on it. Picture yourself disintegrating everything that is on the list. See yourself having dominion over all of your life and that these items are petty nuisance and have no power in your life! Do this until you feel satisfied. Return to sitting. Close your eyes and center yourself with a few deep breaths. Next, either tear up or crumple the list and place in the fire safe container (observing fire safety behavior at all times). Say a releasing prayer or incantation over it.) You can use your own or the following: *"Divine*

Creator, Angels, Guides and Ancestors, give me strength, guidance and protection to release and cancel all negative thoughts and things that I have declared today. So, shall it be. Amen."

Light the list and watch it burn to ash. (*Please use fire safety methods at all times!*) While it's burning, you can recite the releasing prayer as often as you like until it has burned completely. Put the container with the ashes aside. After you close the ritual, the ash can either be flushed in the toilet or buried at the base of a tree. The earth and the tree will recycle and transform the ash into useful energy.

Take your positive list and read it out loud. This is your personalized power affirmations. Keep it handy. You can now close your ritual. Recite a closing prayer. Close the ritual by thanking the Divine Creator, your Spirit Guides and Ancestors for their assistance. Dispose of the ash.

Ground

Once you feel like you're done, take a moment to sit and ground. Feel the surface beneath you supporting you. Imagine that your feet are connected to and rooted firmly in the earth. You can also hold a stone or crystal at this point to connect you with the earth within and without. Pressing your forehead to the ground is another way to ground and root yourself back to the present. When you perform a ritual/ceremony you commune with the astral realm. That is why it is important to ground.

Ritual 3
Clear Negativity with Water

Goal: Cleanse Away Negativity within & without

Timing: Anytime

Frequency: As Needed

What you need: Shower, optional: vase of flowers, incense or oil diffuser, candle.

A simple ritual to release negativity. Water is a powerful element. It is also very receptive to your intentions. In that way you can direct your intentions into the water used in this ritual.

Prepare your bathroom in a way that makes it feel magickal and spiritual. Burn incense or use a diffuser to release a relaxing aroma into the air, light a candle *(always observe fire safety behavior at all times.)* A vase of flowers can add a nice touch brings beauty and refreshes the environment, but is purely optional. Make sure the temperature in the room is comfortable for you. Prepare yourself by going into a meditative state with a few rounds of deep breathing and turning within to that quiet place. Focus on connecting with your inner realm and align with the goal of this ritual. Once you feel relaxed you can begin. Recite an opening prayer. Call on your ancestors, spirit guides to support and protect you in this ritual. Turn on the shower to temperature that is not too hot or too cold (tepid). Sit close by, closing your eyes allow the sound of the falling water to become very prominent. Fix your attention there. Listen to the falling water for a few minutes. Let its sound, rhythm and wetness encompass and relax you. When you feel ready, get into the shower.

Visualize yourself standing underneath a beautiful, magical waterfall. The water is shimmering and extremely bright reflecting the light of the sun giving the appearance of bright silver. It reflects and holds a brilliant light. The water feels alive with positivity and love. It invites you to enter so that it can wash away all that is negative and no longer needed and heal all the places the negativity has touched. Stepping into the falling water the temperature is perfect. The water gently splashes the top of your head and falls to your shoulders and all the way down continuously bathing you in this beautiful shower of illumination. You immediately feel the gloom and weight of negativity falling off into the pool below and disappearing never to return. You can talk to the water and ask it to wash away all that needs to be cleansed away. Talk to the water like you would a friend asking it for help. You can also incorporate any affirmations to recite while in the shower either before, during or after you have been cleansed.

Once you feel the cleansing is complete, say a prayer or affirmations giving thanks. Thank the Creator, Ancestors and Spirit Guides and the Spirit of Water. Know that you have been cleansed of un wanted energies and ready to move forward to manifest!

Note: This ritual can also be done as a visualization if you prefer not going into the shower or can't for whatever reason. I find incorporating the shower to be very powerful and effective. The sounds and the presence of moisture make this a ritual you can strongly feel.

Ritual 4
Manifestation Elixir

Goal: Infuse your intentions into water to become an elixir to take internally

Timing: Anytime

Frequency: Weekly, Daily or at the New Moon

What you need: A drinking glass, a large deep glass bowl (or ceramic can also be used), a lid, saran wrap (or anything you can use to cover the bowl) spring water to fill the bowl, stones: Pyrite, Citrine, Clear Quartz, Moldavite, Lapis Lazuli -- feel free to substitute stones that you prefer, Pencil or pen, Paper

First, script your desires (covered in detail in my first book.) An example is, "I have a thriving business in the field of my dreams, I make tons of money and have great and trustworthy employees." Or, "I am on a beautiful trip to the south of France and staying in luxury hotels, having the most enjoyable time of my life, meeting new and exciting people, seeing all of the best parts of the South of France with plenty of spending money to do whatever I want and plenty left over." Pour your imagination and emotions into the description.

When you are finished, read your script out loud and embody every single aspect of it. Let it be real in your mind down to every cell in your body. Feel the energy of it spread all over you. Place your bowl/container on top of the paper. Then, place your glass inside the bowl and begin to fill it with crystals (leave the quartz crystal for last).

Add the other stones first. As you add each one, hold it to your third eye, then to your heart. Speak to it and ask it to release its most potent power into this manifestation ritual, say what it is for. Feel free to read from a list made in advance. Picking up the clear quartz last, ask for it to harness and intensify the combined power of the stones as well as your intention: Reread or recite out loud what you wrote. Again, visualize and become your statement as you place the clear quartz on top. If you are using a quartz point (tumbled is also fine), make sure the point is facing down, that way the directional energy is heading into the stones and into the container instead of out into space.

Next, pour the spring water into the larger container being careful not to get any water into the glass containing your crystals. Reread/recite out loud the script of your manifestation work as you fill the container with water and place the lid overtop. This time, directly into the water by either putting your hands on the container or leaning over the water and allowing the vibration of your words and your personal energy to go into the water. Allow this elixir to sit for at least 4 hours before drinking. For best results, do this ritual on a full moon and allow the container to sit outside covered overnight to absorb the energy of the moon to enhance the potency of the crystals. However, this is not a necessary step.

You can then drink the water or use it to make manifestation tea (see "Abundance Manifestation Herbs" chapter.) or any beverage of your choosing. Using the same glass of crystals, repeat as desired. Periodically, you want to cleanse and recharge your crystals. You can cleanse them by leaving in the full moon over night or setting in a bowl of sea water. Another method is to smudge them with sage or Palo Santo.

Close the ritual with giving thanks to God, your Ancestors and Spirit Guides, the water, stones and trees (for the paper.) All of these creations are giving energy towards your goal. You can make the elixir as often as you like.

Ritual 5
Water Manifestation Ritual

Goal: Connecting with the element of water to magnify manifestation of desires

Timing: Anytime

Frequency: Daily / Once per week for 1 Month / As desired

What you need: Bath, Clear Quartz Crystal, Epsom Salts, Favorite Essential Oil, White Candle(s)/ Lighter Paper & Pen, Relaxing Instrumental Music

Method: Prepare a calm, relaxing environment in your bathroom by putting on your calming instrumental music. Words distract and direct you towards the theme of the song. You don't want any distractions.

Give thanks to the Divine, call on your Spirit Guides and Ancestors to assist you.

Hold your candle(s) close to your mouth and speak into them prayers or affirmations for abundance and manifestation. Speak from your heart. This is sending the vibration into the candle which acts as an ignition for desires when you light it. Light your candle(s).

Begin to fill the bath with tepid water (room temperature). As the bath fills place your hands under the stream and give thanks for this wonderful element. Talk to the water inviting it in and telling it of your intentions to manifest and that you are calling it forward for its assistance. Once filled, add the salts, oil, and put the clear quartz crystal in the bath (clear quartz is an energy amplifier). Before adding each item, take a brief moment to hold them and thank each item for its assistance. Ask them to ignite their most potent energy into your ritual. Remember everything is alive and has its own form of consciousness. We interact energetically all the time.

Sit at the side of the tub. Close your eyes and focus on the sound of the water stream. Begin to imagine what you want to bring into your current reality. Be as grand, detailed and imaginative as you want. See all that you want pouring into your life easily and effortlessly as the water pours into the tub. See your life being refreshed by all the blessings pouring in and around you. Feel the fullness of it.

Begin to write this version of your life into your journal. As you are writing it, again, see it clearly in your mind in all its splendor and beauty.

Repeat this process until you've written down all the things you want to manifest.

Once you are done, give thanks to the Divine your spirit guides, ancestors, water, fire of the candle, salt, and crystal. Drain the tub. Put out the candle(s). If there is any candle leftover you can save it to relight at bedtime. Note: With candles and fire, always practice fire safety habits.

Every night before bed you can light a white candle and read the list while visualizing. Ensure to add emotional energy into your reading and visualization. Resonate with an unshakable "knowing" that it is so. ***Put the candle out before you go to sleep!***

Ritual 6:
Fifty-five Times Five (55x5) Method

Goal: Intense focus using imagination, written word, spoken word and ancient mathematical activation formula

Timing: Anytime

Frequency: Daily for 5 Consecutive Days

What you need: Pen, Notebook, Fifteen to twenty minutes each day. Optional: candle, incense to create a ritual mood. A quartz crystal to amplify the energy.

Method: Sit at your altar. Light your incense and candle to create a ritual setting. Center yourself with slow, deep breathing and focus on what you are about to do. Get settled. Begin with a prayer. You can also call on your Spirit Guides or Ancestors to bless this ritual before you get started.

In your journal write what you want Fifty-Five Times each day for Five Days, consecutively. After you've finished writing, read your written statement once aloud with emotion, commitment and "know it" as your current reality. Visualize it. Note: I like to sit at one of my altars and do this. You are multiplying and amplifying the energy when you sit at your altar. If you have chosen to include a quartz crystal, I would place the quartz crystal on top of the writing and ask the crystals to intensify your request, or visualize the crystal's energy going into the writing and magnifying its energy.

This method is a layered technique which incorporates three manifestation practices: (1) extended & repetitive mental focus on a desire/intense visualizations, (2) physical action of journaling and, (3) speaking into existence.

This practice directly interacts with your subconscious mind. The more you repeatedly impress upon your subconscious your desires, the more it will acknowledge your desires as truth and will modify your energetic vibration to align with what you desire and to work to bring it into your present reality. Your subconscious will also begin to open you up to inspirations and instructions from your Higher Mind and your Guardian Spirits so that you can clearly identify and act upon the right opportunities and ideas to bring your desires into manifestation as they present themselves to you.

In writing out your desires, be very specific and clear, but also succinct because you are writing them 55 times. I try to fit it into one powerful sentence. Write your desire in the present tense. Know it as though you already have the desired outcome and write in down that way. This will ensure that your subconscious mind receives it in order to take action towards the goal. You will feel very empowered and energetically connected to what you write once you complete the ritual. Immerse yourself in this feeling when it shows up. Remember it to call on whenever you need it. All manifestation and law of attraction work are based off of your mental landscape, emotions and personal energy connecting to the realm of creation. If you miss a day, restart. Focus, take action, and then keep going no matter what.

Ritual 7:
Seventeen 3-6-9 Method

Goal: Bring desires from one reality into current reality

Timing: Once in the Morning, Afternoon & Evening

Duration: 30 days (or until your manifestation)

Frequency: Daily

What You Need: journal or paper, pen. Candle, incense and quartz crystal.

Method: Sit at your altar. Light your incense and candle to create a ritual setting. Center yourself with slow, deep breathing and focus on what you are about to do. Get settled. Begin with a prayer. You can also call on your Spirit Guide or Ancestors to bless this ritual before you get started.

In your journal or on a piece of paper create a statement that describes what you want to manifest. The duration of the single statement must have a writing duration of a minimum of 17 seconds. It can be longer, but not shorter. Write the paragraph three times a day. The first time, write the statement 3 times. The second time, write it 6 times, and the third time, write it 9 times. Do this for 30 consecutive days. If you miss a day, start again. If you have chosen to include a quartz crystal, I would place the quartz crystal on top of the writing and ask the crystals to intensify your request, or visualize the crystal's energy going into the writing and magnifying its energy

This ritual is based on a theory developed by Nikola Tesla. At some point in his scientific career, he realized the universe is made out of energy, vibration, and frequency and that they could be identified in mathematics. He uncovered that the numbers 3, 6, and 9 are numbers that represent the spiritual world, which govern the physical world from the quantum level.

By combining the 3-6-9 code with thought, feelings, and beliefs you will create vibrational frequencies that begin to reshape the universe around you, your physical reality. We constantly resonate vibrationally with our physical and mental realms. By invoking this code, you will be able to influence creation of those things which you want to manifest. By writing the statement each time for a minimum duration of 17 seconds, will ensure that your subconscious mind becomes involved and invested in bringing what you've written about into your current reality.

The 17:3-6-9 Method is similar to the 55x5 method but the principles it is based on are those of Nikola Tesla.

Ritual 8:
Quantum Jumping - Water Technique

Goal: Transmuting current situation from state to desired state.

Timing: First thing in the morning/anytime

Frequency: Once or as often as you feel is needed

What You Need: two glasses or cups, purified or spring water, 2 small pieces of paper the size that will fit on the circumference of the outside of the glasses, pen, tape

This ritual uses water as a conduit to transmute current situations to desired situations. Water is alive and conscious. It takes on the physical shape of whatever you put it in. It also energetically takes on the shape of whatever you impress upon it emotionally and with your focused thought/attention and spoken word. A scientist by the name of Dr. Emoto conducted studies which verified this as fact. Go to this link to read about it.

https://thewellnessenterprise.com/emoto/

Method: Sit at your altar. Light your incense and candle to create a ritual setting. Center yourself with slow, deep breathing and focus on what you are about to do. Get settled. Begin with a prayer. You can also call on your Spirit Guide or Ancestors to bless this ritual before you get started. Announce to them what you are doing and why and that you would like them to add their blessing.

Take two cups/drinking glass (8 oz.). Fill one with drinking water (the best you have-spring, purified or better). On one paper right your current situation (i.e., not working, money is low, undesirable living circumstance, etc.) Tape it to the outside of the glass. On the second piece of paper write your desired situation (i.e., new job working in a great environment doing what I love, lump sum of $1000 showing up to pay bills, perfect apartment with the perfect amount of rent in a perfect neighborhood, etc). Feel free to be detailed, but concise enough to fit on the size paper. Tape it to the other glass. Fill the glass with the current situation with water. Light your candle, light your incense, or start your diffuser with essential oil fragrance. Sit quietly and get into a meditative state. Take the glass with water and pour all of your feelings about your current situation into the water by holding it and thinking about all of what is going on. You can also speak it into the water. After you feel like you have fully activated the water, slowly pour it into the other glass while visualizing your situation changing into your desired situation. Once the second glass is filled, hold it and visualize and speak your new situation into the glass of water. Once you feel you have fully activated the water with your desired situation, state out loud "It is done" three times. Repeat as often as you like. Some people do it once and see results. I would do it a minimum of three consecutive days or until the desired outcome is achieved.

GUIDED MEDITATION
(SELF-HYPNOSIS)

Self-hypnosis / guided meditation are put into ritual format. Instead of just sitting down and going through the process, you will create an ambience of ritual. Dim the lights, light a candle, cleanse the area of unwanted energies with incense or spiritual cleansing water. Call on your Ancestors and Guides to help make your visualization crystal clear with depth, color, 3-D, ... as real as it can be. Ask them to help you travel into that reality and experience it with all of your senses. This style of meditation adds the element of self-hypnosis. The goal is to access your subconscious mind in such a strong way that it begins to overwrite the negative programming that is currently creating obstacles. This will reprogram so that the subconscious aligns and begins to work to manifest your goals. The subconscious responds to most dominant and consistent images, thoughts and beliefs that are it receives and responds to them as being real. Then it works to establish them in your current reality.

The meditation aspect of this ritual connects you to the realm of creation through your crystal-clear visualization which astrally connects you to your unmanifested desires. Remember, the life you want is already created and exists in another realm. Manifestation helps you to magnetize it to your current reality. With this in mind, know that it is available on the astral realm for you to experience through meditation. Once you deeply connect with it in a very realistic and concrete way, it is only a matter of time when it will actualize in your current reality.

This triple component (ritual, self-hypnosis & meditation) is a powerful processs.

Prep: In the meditation there will be a segment where you will take over with your visualization with guiding yourself in visualizing the life you are manifesting. This is an important step to get really clear.

Read each question, then close your eyes and see the answers.

Picture your most perfect day. A day-in-the-life of your ideal life. This should be a day that you could live a variation of over and over. A day that would make you feel blissfully happy.

Where do you live? What is your neighbor like? Feel the feelings you would have as you awake in your ideal location. Perhaps the location is a vacation spot. Go through your morning routine…what does it look like? How do you spend your day? With whom? When do you start your workday or go into your business office? What are your work or business surroundings like? What is your interaction with your coworkers, employees? What is your dream career or business? What kind of conversations are you having? What does the work feel like when you are into it? What are your meals like? Where do you eat. What do you eat? With whom do you eat?

What do you do after work/business is over? Do you meet friends for happy hour? What's the ideal way to spend your early evening? Where do you eat dinner? Do you cook a delicious meal at home or do you go out? Whom do you eat with?

What is your night like? How and with whom do you spend it? What favorite activities do you engage in?

When your day comes to an end and you're ready for sleep what is that like? Do you read, watch tv, play a game? How does it make you feel?

Open your eyes and write it all down. Include your internal feelings, physical feelings, the way the day looks and feels, the weather, temperature, the feel of the clothes your wearing and how the food tasted, the ride to your destinations, the aromas, the levels --- when you walk upstairs, down stairs, in elevators, etc. Try to include every single nuance.

DOESN'T THIS FEEL WONDERFUL?! Hold on to these feelings and feel them as potent energies.

What you will do is take the guided visualization script below and record it on your mobile phone, ipad, or any recording device and insert what you wrote at the appropriate point. You will use this daily (or as often as you like) with ear or headphones. It's important to use your own voice to record. Your voice is the voice your conscious and subconscious mind has been listening to all your life.

Guided Manifestation Meditation Script

"Make sure you're in a comfortable sitting or lying position with your legs and ankles uncrossed. Your arms loose and relaxed at your sides. Now, close your eyes and keep them closed until it is time to open them. Surrender into the surface beneath you. Know that you are fully supported. Relax. Let's take a deep breath, filling your lungs up completely.
Once your lungs are full, let that breath out slowly. Now let's take another deep breath. Once again filling your lungs up completely. And then let that breath out slowly. Let's just take one more very deep breath, filling

your lower and upper lungs completely. Let's hold that breath. Now, let that breath out very slowly. And already you can feel your body just beginning to relax. Just let that wonderful, comfortable feeling of relaxation flow all the way down to your feet.

Keeping the pace steady and slow and putting all of your attention on your breathing. With each outbreath, gently relax your body more and more. Starting with your toes, then your calves, and your knees, next your thighs, lower back, upper back, chest, arms, fingers, neck, face, top of your head. Allow any tension to be released. Feel it fall away. And with each and every breath that you exhale you can feel the muscles in your body relaxing deeper and deeper into a wonderful, comfortable relaxed state.

As you keep going deeper and deeper into this wonderful, relaxed state where you have pleasant, contented thoughts going through your mind and wonderful marvelous feelings flowing all through your whole body, you just keep on going deeper and deeper. All the sounds around you help you keep going deeper and deeper and any sound that you may hear will send you deeper.

As you continue the deep, slow breathing, say to yourself, I embrace abundance in the form of large amounts of material financial wealth. On the out breath, say I release any resistance to abundance. I release all resistance to wealth pouring into my life so that I can help my family, so that I can help my parents, my brothers, my sisters, my friends, my partner. I can bring abundance to any place that I choose.

Now turn deeper within, tap into the realm of creation, the realm of the unlimited source of the universe. Tap into limitless source. Unlimited abundance. The universe is without limits, without boundaries. There is no scarcity where the universe is concerned. Just unlimited love.

I understand and know that whatever I give attention to, I get more of. With the power of intention to create abundance in my life, I turn my mind to the life I am creating…

{{{INSERT YOUR VISUALIZATION HERE}}}

…I know with certainty that the Divine/Universe supports my desires and that my energies have been awakened and aligned in such a way that it activates synchronicity to harmonize with manifesting the life I am calling into being with my visualization. It is so. Amen."

{{{INSERT A COUPLE OF MINUTES OF SILENCE}}}

Begin to slowly bring your awareness back into your body. Begin to move your toes, feel the sensations in your feet as they travel up your body to awaken you. Gently open your eyes."

SPIRITUAL BATHING

A spiritual bath is a standard practice in the spiritual community. Spiritual bathing combines herbs, oils, fresh flowers and other items into water to create an energetic cleansing solution. The bath not only cleanses but also brings a vibration of the desired energy to the bather. The desired energy is determined by the types of herbs, oils and flowers that are used to make it. There are herbs that correspond to every need or desire be it for healing, desired life conditions or spiritual goals. Anyone can create a spiritual bath. I've included below a list of herbs and their properties to choose from to create a spiritual bath.

There are two types of spiritual baths. One is made with a majority of fresh herbs and flowers. A perfume, essential oil or other items may also be added to it. This method will not be discussed here as the process is a little more involved. The other is made with dried herbs, flowers, spiritual curios and essential oils. Spiritual curios (pre-mixed items) are already prepared combination oils or baths that are for specific purposes such as "money drawing, road opener, romance, etc."

Prepare a bath with anywhere from 1 to 5, or more herbs on the list provided by bringing to boil about a 1 to 2 quarts of water. At the boiling point add a teaspoon of each herb (or at least 3 teaspoons of 1 herb), stir and cover. Turn off the flame. Let the herbs steep for 15 minutes. Strain the herbs from the water. Let the herbal solution cool all the way to a comfortable temperature. Add cold water if you need to bring the temperature down. Add a few drops of essential oils that you either like or pertain to the energy of the bath. Not too much essential oil because it can be an irritant. Take a shower or bath to cleanse yourself before you take your spiritual bath. Place the spiritual bath in a bowl or container. After your shower or bath, stand in the tub or shower stall with the container. Close your eyes and pray for what you want. The prayer should invoke the Divine Creator always. If you wish to invoke your spirit guides and ancestors feel free to do so. Slowly pour the spiritual bath down the front and back of your body all the while thinking and visualizing about your desired goal. You can either pour from the top of your head or from the neck down. Once finished towel dry. Enjoy the elevated feeling you have after a spiritual bath. You can use this feeling as an opportunity to engage in a manifestation technique of your choice.

ABUNDANCE MANIFESTATION HERBS

The list of herbs provided in this book are just a few. There is a vast array of herbs that could have been included. However, for this publication the herbs were included for aligning with money, success, abundance, love, luck, protection, happiness and joy. Each herb has several uses and most of the time they are complimentary to the energy you are using it for. Choose what you want to use to make a bath based on the energy. The bath with herbs alone will not be that pleasantly fragrant. Each of the herbs can also be found in essential oil format and you can add a bit of it to make it appealing to you. You can also add another essential oil, perfume or cologne of your choice to give the ath a nice aroma. It is important that this particular bath be pleasing to your senses.

You can also turn the spiritual bath into a **bath ritual**. Instead of pouring the bath over you (recommended for its potency), you can also pour into a tub of warm water, add fresh flowers, light a candle, or dim the lights, pray, play soft, pleasing music and soak for as long as you like. It is important that the bath be warm in temperature because too much heat brings agitation which is an energy that is not harmonious with attracting prosperity and abundance.

A spiritual bath can be taken once (preferably first thing in the morning or in the evening). It is recommended to take a bath for 3, 5 or 7 consecutive days to get a lasting and full effect of the energies of the herbs. Repeating the bath helps to recalibrate your energy frequency.

THE HERBS:

Allspice

Properties: Money, luck, healing, finding treasure, business success, relieves mental tension, and creates a sense of peace and quiet, provides protection, builds courage, and helps make positive changes. It can also help to increase determination to complete a goal, attracts wealth and success, good luck and good fortune, helps make positive changes in general.

Basil

Basil opens the door to transformation. fantastic ingredient for to draw money, protection. attracts money and luck to the home, attracts customers to business, and money to wallets and bank accounts.

Bay Laurel
Other Name: Bay Leaf

Protection, psychic powers, healing, purification, strength, divination, manifestation, prosperity, love, prophetic dreams, success, cleansing, banishing, healing, enhances psychic ability use to bringing about ambitions and goals, luck, success, and abundance, bring about healing and transformation, protection, friendship, gaining what is sought, banishing hostile/negative forces, and mental clarity. purify & raise the spiritual vibrations of an area. Write a wish on a bay leaf and burn it to achieve your goal.

Bergamot

Spiritually, brings balance, restores stability, excellent for strength and protection. Promotes joy.

Chamomile

Ensures good luck and general good fortune attracts money, attracts love, used in sleep and meditation incenses, and associated with riches. It is used to manifest money, peace, love, tranquility and purification.

Cinnamon

Personal and spiritual power, spirituality, healing, success/victory, protection, love, luck, lust, strength, and prosperity, draws money and success.

Cloves

Protection, Exorcism, Love, Money, gaining what is sought, banishing hostile/negative forces, brings mental clarity, attracts riches, purifies & raises spiritual vibrations of an area, draws wealth and prosperity, ensure that your manifestation intention is realized.

Ginger

Used for manifestation to come into fruition faster, as well as enhancing the potency of the process. It is also used to enhances passion in relationships.

Marjoram

Attracts love and happiness, money, healing and health, peace, protection calm sleep, joy, wishes, and psychic enhancement.

Mint

Restores hope, revives the mind, gets us moving. Mint commands us to thrive, makes manifestation work faster, or to better prepare your mind and intentions to be aligned with the intentions of a manifestation process. Mint reminds us not to lose hope; we can thrive and prosper, no matter what our current growing conditions may be.

Parsley

Enhances clairvoyance, cleansing, consecration, contacting other planes, fertility, good luck, invocation, meditation, supports change and transition, Enhances lust, brings good luck, communicating with other planes, protection, purification, fertility, strength, vitality, divination, passion, meditation, rituals for the dead, and happiness.

Patchouli

Great for money manifestation, potent ingredient with money and prosperity rituals. Enhances sex, love and attraction. The oil can be sprinkled onto money, added to purses and wallets, and placed around the base of green candles. It is commonly added to love sachets and baths.

Thyme

Purifies, increases psychic powers, opens 3rd eye, increases strength and courage. Enhances mindset to achieving goals that seems un-achievable, helps keep a positive attitude.

OTHER TYPES OF RITUALS

Group Manifestation Rituals

I love working solo, but nothing replaces the wonderful dynamics of group energy. A coming together of people who are on a similar path is extremely powerful and effective. Group energy can be focused to support each individual's overarching goals. The manifestation ritual can be done in person or over the internet via zoom or skype. It can also be done in a private group via Facebook live. I prefer zoom because it allows for everyone to be seen and heard during the ritual. That way you can communicate back and forth with the group or even privately to another member via chat. The host can also share their screen with everyone if there is something for the group to be able to view. Leading up to and after the ritual, the group can stay in touch to encourage each other, share valuable insights and tips that have been learned along the way.

Gratitude Ritual

Last, but definitely not least is a Gratitude Ritual. Gratitude is the single most powerful manifesting energetic tool in the whole of abundance principles.

A daily gratitude practice creates an energetic field that attracts abundance. Your gratitude is the energy that builds the magnetic force of attracting abundance. Being grateful is important in abundant times and especially if you're experiencing scarcity. Small acts of gratitude such as notes to loved ones of how much they mean to you. Notes and gestures of thanks to those who have been there for you, are great ways of showing gratitude to your immediate circle. A note, a text, a card, an email, a phone call do not cost much more than a few minutes of time. Reciting or writing down what you are grateful for can be done daily to lock in your gratitude mindset.

On a grander scale, you can perform a Gratitude Ritual. This involves setting up a small altar and giving prayerful thanks and offerings to the Divine and spirits that support you such as your ancestors and spirit guides, etc. If you already have your altars, then that is half of the work already done.

Prep: Take time to write down a separate letter to your ancestors and spirit guides. Prepare an offering of a few of the foods (fruits, pastries, cooked food) that they favor, purchase a bouquet of flowers, a candle the color that represents them or white, burn incense or an essential oil in a diffuser to create sweet aroma. Sweetness attracts good spirits. Setup everything on the altar, arranging it nicely so that it is appealing to the eye. Connect intuitively to see if there is anything else that is needed. The ancestors and most guides were people who lived on earth, so they do have items that they like.

Before starting any ritual, spiritually cleanse the area you will be doing with incense (sage, frankincense, Palo Santo, etc.) to eliminate unwanted energies and to bring in pleasing and calm energies. Prepare yourself mentally and go into a meditative state.

Dim the lights. Light your altar candle. Burn the sweet incense or essential oil. Open with a prayer of thanks to the Supreme Being / God / Goddess (whichever is your practice). Then proceed with prayers to the ancestors first. Invite them to join you in this celebration of thanks. Do the same for your spirit guides. Read your letters of thanks out loud and with heart, reverence, joy and fun. Play the music you feel would match with your ritual. Dance if you feel it. Go with the flow. Connect with them and intuit how things should go. Once you feel the ritual should come to a close, say another prayer of general thanks and release your ancestors from the ritual by thanking them and letting them know the celebration has come to a close. Give thanks to the Divine. Close the ritual. You can journal about your experience to seal it in.

You will find that when you participate in these acts of gratitude, you are reminded that you already have all that you need to not only get by, but to thrive. All the skills, talents and knowledge are already inside of you waiting to be applied, as well as all the energies are aligned, good spirits are helping and supporting you.

ADDITIONAL MANIFESTATION TOOLS

Emotions & Evidence Board

An Emotions and Evidence Board revolves around displaying the "reasons" for what you want to achieve and the "evidence" of what you have already achieved. This will help to evoke positive emotions that are bursts of energetic power that can be used to fuel your manifestation work. The emotions element further underlines your "reasons" for desiring the manifestations that you want to achieve. Abundance is magnetized more powerfully when your reasons also include the benefit of others. This makes this manifestation for the good of many and not just one. The evidence element confirms to you, what you are capable of achieving. Collect copies of photos the evoke powerfully positive memories—fun, joy, accomplishment, love, family & loved ones. Also, include photos of times that you are proud of having achieved. Remember you are already a Manifestor so you have evidence. If photos are hard to come by, print out statements of what you've accomplished or what brings you joy. Take either poster board or art board and create a collage. Ritualize the creative process by lighting a candle, burning incense or using an oil diffuser to release aromas that invigorate, saying an invocation / prayer or affirmations that place you in a positive and powerful mindset. Look at each picture or read each saying with deep reverence. Connect to those moments powerfully, register all the good emotions that they bring up. Seal in these emotions so that they can seep into your physical and spiritual DNA. Try to be as decorative and artsy as you can in creating the board so that it is eye pleasing to you. Your skill level doesn't matter. Do what you can. After it's finished you can put in an area where you will see it regularly.

When you have completed the ritual. Thank the Divine, Spirit Guides and Ancestors and also give thanks to all of the memorable successes you have been able to honor with this ritual. Close the ritual with a prayer or affirmation. Put out the candle. Put the board where you will be able to see it regularly. If you're not able to do this, pull it out regularly to focus on when doing manifestation work. It is a good starter to bring up the emotional power that you can pour into the work that you do.

This board is a powerful tool to release the negative that show up. It will immediately give you the ability to turn your thoughts to positivity.

Acknowledge the Little & Big Wins Along Your Journey

Acknowledging even the slightest manifestations along the way sends out positive energy and gratitude to the universe. Be aware of the little gains as this sends a signal to your higher self that you are grateful. The acknowledgement can be a simple prayer when you receive an expected or unexpected increase. Perhaps you go to purchase something that you are expecting to pay $20.00 for, but when you get to the store it is on sale for $12.99. That's a win! A smile to yourself and thanking the Creator is good enough. You can also celebrate by sharing with others that are on a similar path so that they can encourage and affirm you.

A celebration ritual can be used when you reach a milestone on your manifestation path, but it can also be used to remind yourself to celebrate your full potential and value! Use your imagination. Have fun!

Create A Manifestation Schedule

Schedule your manifestation processes throughout the day, week, month and try your best to stick to it. I personally have hourly small rituals that I do. Others are on a monthly, weekly or daily schedule. Repetition is important in this work.

Create A Manifestation Altar

Create a manifestation-abundance altar will create an energy center that will further enhance your manifestation work. It acts as place where you can consistently go to do your manifestation rituals. Overtime it builds an accumulation of energy that is tuned into your goals and aspirations. I cover this in my previous book, "The Art of Manifestation: Simple Energy Techniques to Creating the Life You Deserve," available on Amazon, https://lnkd.in/eZmuNzY.

Create Personal Wealth Corner

If you're not into setting up an altar, a wealth corner maybe an option for you. It is a small space that contains symbols of wealth and prosperity. It can be decorative and it will blend into the house décor. Much like the altar, it will build up energy and attract what you are working on. The main difference is that it is not "working space" like the altar.

Give the Blessing of Abundance

Giving to those in need and who are less fortunate or going through a difficult time is an honorable act. It indicates a loving, giving heart that understands that we are all connected. It doesn't have to be in money. It can be in time or giving the value of some of the work that you are already doing to someone who could use it. Only do this if you really feel it in your heart. Doing this just because you want to gain wealth and prosperity is not only shady, but the universe knows the difference.

Sleeping on a Bed of Prosperity

Create a wealth tray and place items of prosperity and abundance on it and place them under the bed. This is a subtle energy technique. When we are sleeping, we are traveling into the astral plane. We are very keen and receptive to energies. Everything on earth has a spiritual counterpart that is visible on the astral plane. By having this bundle of prosperity items under your bed, your spirit will notice them and the energy will be subtly reinforced in your subconscious. Remember, it's about layering and enforcing what you are manifesting in different ways. Periodically, clean and swap out items as you see fit. While seemingly simple, it may just change your life and help you manifest an effortless prosperity you desire!

Prosperity in Your Wallet

Place crystals that enhance prosperity in your wallet. The following crystals attract success and abundance: citrine, green aventurine, pyrite, malachite. They are sold in small sizes to fit in your wallet or pocketbook. You can also place these crystals on your desk at work, business office or cashier area, nightstand, etc. You can also make a sachet (draw string pouch) with a combination of the herbs listed above to carry in your wallet.

Prosperity Cologne
(Simple Recipe)

You can make a simple prosperity cologne to keep around to refresh yourself, your wallet / pocketbook or your prosperity altar. The recipe is the following:

1 bottle of Florida Water
A pinch of ground cloves
5 drops basil oil
Pinch of dry thyme
5 drops of honey
A pinch of ground allspice
3 drops of ginger essential oil
3 drops of peppermint oil

Pour the Florida Water into a bowl and add all the ingredients. Return to the bottle or fill into another bottle and cap it keep handy to use as needed. Florida Water can be purchased at your Dollar Store or neighborhood Botanica. It is a well-known Spiritual Water this is widely used in the Spiritualist and Lucumi traditions for cleansing and uplifting people's energy. It is also used in spiritual baths. You can add it to any of the baths provided in this book to boost up the effectiveness. By adding the suggested ingredients to it, ensures that it will work for prosperity.

Attraction Oil
(This oil can be used to bring things to you, in this case, prosperity and abundance)

Ingredients:

Essential Oils: Lovage, cinnamon, sweet orange, lemon

Lemon peel and dry or fresh

1 oz Almond oil

1 oz clean dropper bottle

Directions: Combine 10 drops of each essential oil of: Lovage, cinnamon, sweet orange oil, lemon oil into 1 oz of almond oil into a bowl. Add lemon peel and place the lodestone and pyrite in the mixture. Cover and let it sit overnight. Best done during the New Moon. Let sit outside in the New Moon if possible. Remove stones and pour mixture into the dropper bottle. Ask your Spirit Guides and Ancestors to bless the mixture. Let it sit on your altar overnight. Double blessed oil. Use to anoint candles, self, wallet/purse, use in diffuser or on anything you want to attract. Say your intentions.

ENERGY…again

We are created by the One Source/God. We are made up of energy. Everything is made of up energy. Energy cannot be destroyed. It only changes form. It shifts to other states of being. As energetic beings we have the ability to take advantage of the different stages of our energy for every aspect of life. Life is all energy. Every created and yet to be created thing is connected through energy. Everything comes from this energy and returns to it. Each culture has given its own name to it, but it is essentially the same with minor variations of cultural and spiritual perspectives. It is through this energetic connection that we are able to influence and manipulate. With this knowledge we are empowered to direct certain areas of our lives and create different opportunities. This fundamental fact is important to any manifestation work. Developing your ability to energetically align with what you desire is tantamount. It is the main ingredient of manifestation. It is foundational in the Law of Attraction. Like energy attracts like energy. When you begin to see that everything is energetically alive, you will begin to embrace the world differently. You will be able to understand, more and more, your connection to your environment and everyone around you. This enables you to sense, feel and mentally log energetic resonances so that this catalog of information is readily available to use in your manifestation work.

Visiting locations that you want to live gives you the direct energetic experience that you can file away mentally to call upon when you are working on manifesting. Placing yourself in environments that you would like to make a frequent part of your life experience is another way to get the energetic experience to file in your mental toolbox. Visiting dealerships and test-driving cars you wish to own will allow you to directly experience the energy of it and file it mentally for use in your manifestation work. Everywhere you go that uplifts and inspires you, be keenly aware of the experience and the way it makes you feel so that you can reproduce it in your visualizations not only the visual aspect, but the emotional and energetic feel of it. Also, whenever you personally have an experience that brings you happiness and joy, take a moment to immerse yourself fully into those feelings and then mentally file away the energetic make up of it. The emotions that are felt during this experience are types of energetic experiences that enhance manifestation. The emotions of joy, happiness, laughter are directly aligned to and will attract abundance. You want to be able to call upon this energy when needed. Your ability to compile file with various energetic signatures will come in handy for your manifestation work.

Primordial Source/Force is where all creation originates. In essence, it is Primordial Energy. Everything is made from the primordial source which means all uncreated and created life (animate and inanimate) has consciousness because it originates from this primordial source. Energetically, everything in the material realm has a counterpart in the spiritual realm. It was first created there before it existed here. Everything that has yet to be created exists in an unmanifested form in the realm of the formless. The herbs, crystals, oils and ritual items discussed in this book are all made up of energy resonating at various rates. When you combine them for a specific purpose, you are combining the energy resonances together to create a new more diverse and powerful resonance. This new powerful resonance will be directed into action by your intentions.

Nurturing & Building Up Your Personal Energy for Spiritual Work

All human beings are incarnated into this world as spiritual beings housed in physical bodies. Your spirit and physical body work together to resonate your own unique vibrational energy. This is your core energy. Your "home" energy. Your soul energy. This is the energetic frequency that makes you unique. The next step is learning how to manage your energy and build it up.

All ritual work and work involving the making of spiritual oils, baths and incenses is infused with your energy. It is your energy that unlocks and activates the deeper levels of energy within the materials being used. That is why in some cases spiritual baths, oils and incenses made by some are not as effective. The energies of the herbs and materials being used is subtle. Your personal energy is what boosts up the effectiveness.

Handling Negative Thoughts

Negative energy can counter your manifestation goals. Your mindset is the most crucial because it is the source of how you create your life. Negative mindset, doubt, depression, anxiety, anger, etc. are not conducive to creating a better life. Most people are not able to be positive all of the time, but for the majority of the time is where you want to be. I cover this topic in detail in my previous book, *"The Art of Manifestation: Simple Energy Techniques to Creating the Life You Deserve,"* available on Amazon, https://lnkd.in/eZmuNzY. You can also research how to manage emotions and negative mindset with other sources. It is important to be working on this either before or at the onset of your manifestation work. However, adding it anytime is better than not at all.

POTENTIALITY & THE GATEWAY OF MANIFESTATION

Our inner potential makes us who we are as humans. It is always just beneath the surface for us to tap into to manifest our desires. It is this potential that is the force all of life draws on to manifest. It is also responsible for our ability to continuously exceed top performance levels in every area of life. It is the root power of manifestation.

An obvious example is in the world of sports when athletes continue to exceed beyond the world records, setting new ones. Athletes are continuously excelling beyond what was previously the highest performance level. The realm of potential is a crucial part of how these breakthroughs happen. With a strong desire, mindset, training, and visualization athletes are able to access this realm of potential to accomplish their goals. They do it instinctively, for the most part. You don't have to know about it to access it. We were all born with the instinct to tap into this power.

Human potential exists at a level that is called "mind level." However, potentiality is all around us in the galaxy and in all of life (seen and unseen). Everything that has ever existed in the world existed first in the formless realm of potentiality. Like gravity. It is a force that is of great importance to existence, but it is not visible. There is immense power in it.

Most of us unconsciously draw from this realm of potentiality throughout our lifetime. For the purpose of intentional manifestation, we can consciously connect with this realm to create the life we desire and deserve. There is an inner access point, a gateway, where potential meets manifestation. This is the point where we can bring things or conditions into being.

Manifestation techniques must be accompanied by action on your part. These techniques work best when they have lines of energetic and physical avenues that are already in place or are being built into place. So, if you want a thriving business, then you have to have business plans or a business in place that the energy can link with and move it into fuller manifestation, etc. Forethought and actions always go hand in hand with it. They are powerful partners.

PUTTING IT ALTOGETHER

When you begin to approach manifestation as a part of your daily life, you can develop ways in which to incorporate the practices creatively and in a way that makes sense for your schedule and your life. Once you familiarize yourself with all of the rituals and techniques you should decide which ones appeal to you most. Once you've determined this, you should then map out a daily, weekly and monthly schedule. Most people assign certain practices to the morning and evening which makes it easier to schedule around work and family obligations. Other people who have more flexible schedules can set a schedule to implement these techniques throughout the day in the morning, afternoon and evening. The most minimal schedule should be once per day either in the early morning upon rising or in the late evening before bed. The most important thing is to setup a schedule that will be easy to keep. Repetition is one of the key elements of ensuring your techniques will bring you what you want.

Layering is another consideration in the process of manifestation. What I mean by that is to make sure to include different techniques that emphasize activating energy in different ways such as: visualizing (visual), affirmations (spoken word), Act As If (emotions), Scripting (written word), prayer & gratitude (spirit). Doing this will ensure that you are operating your manifestation skills on all levels (multi-layered). This aids in bringing manifestation quicker and with a lasting presence in your life. Some of the rituals already incorporate all of these layers, but rituals are scheduled at intervals (monthly, weekly, during the full or new moon cycles, etc.) You want to layer your manifestation techniques on a daily basis. The items that take a shorter amount of time you can do daily, the rituals and other techniques that are more lengthy, can be scheduled weekly or monthly.

CONCLUSION

When you focus every morning and every night on the deliberate creation of a certain reality, it is your spirit that adds the power and energetic spark. There is a deep, next level commitment to the deliberate manifestation of your desired reality.

The Art of Manifestation is a beautiful way to develop yourself spiritually and awaken you to the mysteries within and the mysteries without. It is exciting and challenging all rolled into one. It is an involved process that requires deep focus, commitment and lots of patience. It also requires flexibility of perspective and expectations. What is very specific to manifesting an abundant life is that you must rely heavily on the unseen realm and delve into it to discover where your personal entry point is to this magical and mystical realm of creation. You hone your skills and learn how YOU, specifically, go within and call up and direct your energetic signature to magnetize and pull in what it is you want for your life. Another interesting point along this journey is you are required to become clearer and clearer about your values and what truly brings you happiness and fulfillment. The energetic forces that you tap into brings a realization of the power that resides in the Universe and it is nothing to take for granted. You learn that you only want to use this energy to bring in good and beneficial things that will touch not only your life but the lives of your loved ones and cascade out to your community as well. You also learn that Love is the language of the Universe. The Universe is ready and willing to abide and provide.

I hope the rituals, ceremonies, incense, oils, tips and techniques help you along your manifestation journey. Combined with the manifestation principles detailed in my earlier book, *"The Art of Manifestation: Simple Energy Techniques to Creating the Abundant Life You Deserve,"* you will have two books that provide complementary information that will be able to assist you in being successful.

I hope you've enjoyed the material presented in this book. Happy Manifesting!

Special Thanks

This work would not be complete without mentioning the unending support and encouragement by some very special people in my life. First, my daughter, Tehja A. Fagains, whose vision of me I continue to hold and strive towards. She is my rock and my biggest encourager. She inspires me and is the reason I continue to move forward on my path. Her faith in my work keeps me grounded and on course. She also designed the photoshoot for the cover, took the photos and did an amazing makeup look! My big sister, Denise Phillips, who is always there to cheer me on, support me and she also helped me edit this work. She is one of the people I look up to most! A brilliant mind and a sweet spirit. My other big sister, Yvette Jackson, who is a light and love that is always there to nurture and lift me up. She reminds me of the beauty that resides within. I also am supremely thankful for the love and support of my spiritual sisterhood that surrounds me—Kathleen Bullock, Gladys Wrenick and Amy Fabrikant, whom I can always count on for love, advice and insight. Last but certainly not least, my Coach and Mentor, Abiola Abrams, who continuously, guides, inspires and challenges me to discover my best self and to translate that part of me to those whose lives I touch. Her spiritual and business tools are incomparable!

About the Author

Rev. Mignon Grayson is the Founder of Sacred Mysteries World Wide and an ordained Interspiritual Indigenous Faith Minister of One Spirit Interfaith Seminary in New York City. She was ordained in 2016. She chose the interfaith path due to her calling to serve people of all faiths and religious practices. Mignon recognizes that there is a common link to the Divine Creator within all religious traditions.

She is a devotee of the Ifa Orisha tradition of Nigeria and initiated as a Yayi (Priestess) in Palo Mayombe, rooted in Congo spiritual traditions. As a result of her spiritual journey, Mignon has learned the deep importance of the ancestors and their connection to daily life and spiritual evolution. Ancestral reverence is an inherent core practice throughout most ancient cultures. Mignon's particular focus is to bring the wisdom of ancient spiritual traditions from across the world to the masses through Sacred Mysteries World Wide with classes, lectures, symposiums and creating on-going conversations about spirituality and its primary importance in evolving and healing the planet.

As a spiritual evolutionary coach, Mignon seeks to inspire and support people on their spiritual journey by assisting them in connecting with their most authentic and sacred soul expression. As a sound healer, Mignon uses the vibrational energies of sound to bring about healing by energy recalibration. She works passionately to be a constant vessel of healing, love and spirituality.

Please go to the link below to leave a review of this book on Amazon:

https://www.amazon.com/dp/B07ZZLS5ST

Other Books by the Author:

**The Art of Manifestation:
Rituals, Crystals, Herbs, Oils & Baths to Create the Abundant Life You Deserve**

Stay connected! Sign Up for our Blog.

www.sacredmysteries.org/signup

Links

rev_mignon@sacredmysteries.org

Follow us on Instagram @sacredmysteries_ww

Checkout the blog at our website: www.sacredmysteries.org/blog

Facebook: Sacred Mysteries Worldwide

YouTube Channel: Sacred Mysteries World Wide

We Are Always Here to Help!

Just getting started on your spiritual path? Click the links below to our YouTube channel which has videos that can help you on your journey:

Sacred Mysteries World Wide YouTube Channel:

https://www.youtube.com/channel/UCpgEudpK0Rhs3KaPii7ZIaw

Cont'd – links to Youtube videos:

"Tips for Beginning on A Spiritual Path"
https://youtu.be/KoxmNyaIxLg

"Getting Started Meditating – The Basics"
https://youtu.be/AtY_a4gCdBY

"Beginning Meditation 2 – Chanting"
https://youtu.be/j2wDKmFROVs

"Ancestors: How to Honor, Connect & Setup an Altar"
https://youtu.be/PKKxv8-h3JY

"How to Create an Ancestor Altar *Simple*
https://youtu.be/IVWJI7HQMBc

Printed in Great Britain
by Amazon